The Book of
GEORGE

Published by
Write Impression Ltd.
ISBN 978-0-473-60187-4

Dear Cat Lovers,

Over the years, I've shared my life with many cats. We've not only successfully fostered hundreds of cats and kittens, but we've also had quite a few "foster fails" along the way, all of whom joined the family permanently. Many of our beloved feline companions have graduated from life on Planet Earth and have been recalled to Planet Cat (a.k.a. Heaven) to serve as angels. This tribute to George is a fundraiser for Feline Fix.

Part One is a true account of how George came to join our family, and how we surmise he was dispatched from it after only two short years. Carefully note that this is pure speculation on our part as we have no concrete evidence of how he died. Part Two is the imagined story of George's journey to find us. This is mostly fiction. We have no idea where he went or what he did in the eight months between leaving his family and finding us.

I hope you enjoy his story. I have also created several other books as fundraisers for various cat charities.

You can reach me by email and I'd love to hear from you:

cats@deanes.co.nz

I'm also on Facebook:

facebook.com/TheNotSoCrazyCatLady

Linda Deane

"With heartfelt thanks to all of you who support and care for your own cats and for the less fortunate felines. Planet Cat blesses you with much kitty-love, purrs and head boops."

HRH George Stuart Deane the First

Part 1
The End and the Beginning

George mysteriously appeared in our garden on a winter day in June 2019. At first, we assumed he belonged to someone new to the neighbourhood and was simply exploring new territory. I tried to befriend him as I do with any cats I meet, but he was wary of me and ran off whenever I approached. I didn't pay that much attention to him, as our little cat, Sparkles, was not well at the time and we had other major issues going on.

As time passed, George started spending more and more time in our garden. Sometimes I noticed an almost identical cat accompanying him, so alike I

I've heard bacon is served at this establishment, Linda.

thought they were siblings. George's friend came and went, but George appeared to take up residence. He didn't look lost or hungry,

My best mate.

so I refrained from feeding him because I thought he had a home and I didn't want to encourage someone else's cat to move in with us. Nevertheless, he seemed to be sleeping on the chair outside our patio slider.

I managed to take a few reasonable photographs which I posted on Facebook in several community and missing animal groups, but nobody responded. I checked Neighbourly and all the local notice boards for missing cats. Again nothing, so I put an old blanket in a box and left it on our patio where he could get a bit more shelter and a comfy spot to nap. I saw that he was using it, but he continued to stubbornly reject any other overtures I tried.

On July 1st, 2019, our beloved Sparkles was recalled to Planet Cat (a.k.a. Heaven). Our kindly vet made a house call to carry out her euthanasia, and she crossed over cradled in her favourite human's arms, finally free of all pain and suffering. I let the vet out and left Mr. Deane to grieve privately as he sat on the bed still cuddling the lifeless body of his little soul-cat. I wandered around in the garden for a short while then sat down on the bench to vent my own grief. George kept his distance but stayed with me.

Next morning, we buried Sparky in view of our bedroom window. I lingered in front of the sad little grave with its freshly planted *Daphne odora*, telling myself that the fragrance of Daphne would always remind me of her. I was lost in thought and replaying scenes from Sparky's kittenhood when I became aware of something warm and soft brushing against my legs. Our cats are indoor only, and so I was quite startled.

I looked down, and George was standing right beside me and looking up at me as if to say, "It's all right: I'm here for you." Without thinking, I scooped him into my arms and cried into his silky white and grey fur. He didn't offer the slightest resistance and, after I had cried myself out, allowed me to carry him inside with me. I put him down and he strolled about our kitchen as if he'd always been there. I gave him a meal and he ate it heartily while Callie glared at him balefully from the doorway before joining him.

Our Callie has quite a foul mouth and did not take kindly to him at first. She swore at him using the most colourful, unladylike language imaginable: lots of Fs and Ss passed her lips as she hissed and spat at him in Catlish. Fortunately for me, I don't understand much Catlish or Felinese, but judging by the tone she used, I would probably have been quite shocked. George simply ignored it, strolled into the dining room, and curled up for a nap on the carpet in the puddle of sun by the window.

Before letting him out that afternoon, I made a paper collar with our phone number and a message for his owners informing them that their cat appeared to have adopted us, but that they were welcome to come and claim him. By 7PM he was back, sitting outside the patio slider and politely asking to come in. Since it was cold and windy, I let him in and he settled on the couch for an evening of Netflix with us as we tried to take our minds off the loss of Sparky.

Once again, Callie was not at all pleased with this encroachment on her territory. As undisputed Queen of the household, this part of the house had been her exclusive domain. Candy, the late Sparky and the Outpawed kids (Miss Madelyn (aka Moppy) and Vlad) lived on the other side, separated by a closed passage door to keep the "peasants" confined to their own quarters.

Her Majesty does not get on well with the others and takes every opportunity to tell them what low-born trash they are when compared with *her* impeccable Calico-Siamese lineage.

Mr. Deane slid the patio door open at bedtime and invited George to leave, but he politely declined and sought permission to keep the Queen company overnight. Since we know that the Queen's bark is far worse than her bite, we thought it would be all right: George had shown no sign of aggression and he was a big, muscular boy who could defend himself if she tried to slap his face. As it was a cold and blustery night, we let him persuade us to have it his way.

I've no idea what he said or did during the night to convince Her Majesty that he was worthy of her attention. Up until then, she had not shown the slightest connection with any cat since she'd said goodbye to her two ladies in waiting, Katie and Pookie, a few years before, but Mr. Deane found the two of them in the kitchen the next morning, sitting amicably side by side and waiting for breakfast. After his initial disappointment that bacon was not on the menu, George tucked into a hearty breakfast with Callie.

Later that morning, we took him to the vet to be scanned for a microchip. George was indeed microchipped, but the chip had not been registered on the database and the vet was pessimistic that we would be able to find his people. Mr. Deane is not a man to give up easily, however. With some research, he discovered that George's chip had been part of a batch allocated to the Wellington SPCA in March of of 2013. He rang them and discovered that George had indeed been chipped at 8 weeks old. Wellington SPCA had also recorded his adoption and promised to contact his people to pass on our details.

A few days later, we received a call from Waikanae Beach. We live about 5 kilometres inland. The caller informed us that while she had been living in Otaki (which is about 20 kilometres from Waikanae), George had simply upped and disappeared eight months earlier. George's erstwhile family had subsequently moved to Waikanae Beach.

It turned out that the family had adopted a puppy and George, being a very staid, calm sort of cat, had found the boisterous puppy too much to handle, so he had simply left. The family came around to claim George on the afternoon of 8th July 2019, bringing their baby, a rowdy pre-school child and the boisterous, equally rowdy dog. George was clearly stricken as he recognised them through the glass panel at the front door and bolted for safety behind the couch.

Much to my horror, the child, oblivious to his mother's feeble instruction to calm down, shrieked after George, grabbed him by his back legs and dragged him out from behind the couch while the dog barked and pranced in a frenzy. I managed to rescue George from the fracas and scooped him up onto my shoulder where he clung in terror, safely out of their reach.

Meanwhile, Mr. Deane had been trying to get coherent information from the father. He confirmed that it was indeed George and casually stated, "Oh, he looks happy enough. You can have him if you want him."

Mr. Deane and I agreed immediately and hustled mother, father, baby, child and dog out the door as fast as possible before the wailing child persuaded the parents otherwise. The mum shoved the poor dog into the boot of her sedan, and for a second I thought she was going to toss the child in too, but he clambered into the back seat in a rage, slamming the door so hard our kitchen windows rattled.

It was the last we heard of them, and that was how George officially came to be our cat, bringing our total back to five exactly one week after we said goodbye to Sparky. I think Sparky knew we were going to need George and had orchestrated it all.

George lived peacefully with Callie on her side of the house, while Candy, Moppy and Vlad lived on the other. We would have preferred George to be an indoor cat like the others, but he was miserable if we didn't allow him out to patrol the garden perimeter.

We reluctantly let him out after breakfast every day, whereupon he would do his circuit and settle on his patio chair for its outlook over the garden, and there he would snooze for most of the day whilst keeping an eye on things.

When I happened to be working in the garden, he would always assist me, doing his best to hamper my every move. If I was pulling up weeds, he would flop down on the patch where I was working and roll about to flatten the weeds for me. He had a way of butting my hands with his head just as I was planting

a delicate seedling and sending it flying. He also liked helping to dig the holes for these seedlings. He was very enthusiastic and took his duties as my gardening assistant seriously.

This garden is like Linda: high-maintenance.

My fence.
My tree.
My bench.
My chair.

He was also thoroughly committed as my bodyguard. Under no circumstances was I ever permitted to walk down our long driveway to fetch the mail without him, and he would walk with me every time to protect me from the vicious and unpredictable Cocoa, a neighbouring cat who is known to lie in wait under hedges to launch Ninja attacks on unsuspecting ankles.

In the months that followed, George spent all but the coldest and wettest days enjoying the fresh air from the comfort of his chair by the patio door, napping or assisting me as required. At about 4PM he would ask to be let in, and then Callie would yell at him like an old fishwife in a manner completely

unbecoming of her royal status before washing his face and accompanying him to the kitchen where they'd both enjoy a snack before teatime.

Callie and George loved each other dearly. I have cared for hundreds of cats, and I've never seen a bond between two who aren't littermates like the one between Callie and George. They slept in the same bed, groomed each other and were never physically far apart. Like any married couple, they had their differences. Callie's quick temper and colourful vocabulary would sometimes get the better of her, but George took it all stoically – until he'd had enough. At times like these, he'd slam-dunk her to the ground with one blow of a powerful front paw, then be instantly repentant, but it always had the required effect: she was shocked into behaving herself and then they would immediately kiss and make up, grooming each other's faces before cuddling up together for a nap in their favourite spot, on top of the couch backrest. This leather couch has sustained permanent damage from their combined weight!

During the short time George was with us, foster fails Judi, Poddy, Quaddy and Nixie joined our family in quick succession. George's easy-going and friendly nature ensured he got on well with everyone, but he preferred the company of his Queen and chose to continue living on her side of the house.

George was the gentlest of giants. He never caught birds or hunted anything bigger than a cicada. I often wondered how he had survived eight months as a travelling cat until he demonstrated just how swiftly he could dispatch those annoying insects with a swipe of his paw and a crunch of his jaw. I also observed him slurping up earthworms when I was gardening, but he never showed any interest in birds. I think it requires a certain amount of agility and stealth to catch birds. George's robust physique and solid build was more suitable for hunting larger prey such as rabbits.

George stayed on our property. It seemed that once he found the home he wanted, he was not a wandering sort. Sometimes he liked to catch the late afternoon sun from a perch on the top of the boundary fence, and to do this, he'd wriggle under the fence and climb it from the neighbour's side as it was much easier to get to the top that way. This is as far as he would stray from our property.

Content Warning:

Please skip the following paragraphs if you are a sensitive reader and resume reading at the next heading.

At around 4PM on 9th June 2021, I stepped outside to call him in. Something was wrong. He was always waiting to come in at around this time, after which he would remain inside until after breakfast the next day, but not this time. George was nowhere to be seen.

Mr. Deane reported that he'd last seen him at around 2PM sunning himself on our driveway.

I searched for him, walking around the garden, checking along the boundary fence. I called, but there was no answer. This was so unlike George's usual behaviour that I started to panic. I walked around our neighbourhood calling for him, but there was still no sign. I went out again at about 6PM and did another patrol of the garden. It was then that I found him, lying face down in a flower bed against the fence with his back foot wedged in the bottom slats.

He most certainly had not been there when I was looking for him earlier. There was no sign of a struggle which is what I might have expected if his foot had been caught in the fence for real. George was a big, powerful boy and would have struggled for his freedom and would also have called for help which Mr. Deane would certainly have heard from his quiet home office. Plants and soil around his body were completely undisturbed, and his front legs were tucked neatly along his flanks – he hadn't even moved them forward to brace himself. His body was ice cold and rigor mortis had set in.

We have no proof, so this is purely speculation, but I'm almost convinced the scene was staged to make it look like an accident prior to me coming out to look for him a second time. All the signs point to a nasty neighbour who does not like cats. We suspect he killed George earlier, probably soon after he was seen in our driveway. He had most likely wriggled under the fence to climb up the other side and enjoy the afternoon sun when he was brutally kicked in the back of the head by a steel capped boot and left to lie against the fence until it was dark enough to throw his lifeless body over without being seen. I am

no vet, but his neck felt broken when I examined him afterwards. Our only comfort is that his death must have been swift and that there were no other signs of injury or suffering.

George was not a roamer or a trespasser. His time with us was a short two years.

Beloved Georgie Pie, we were so unprepared for this. I thought you would be with us for many, many years to come and we all miss you terribly, but Callie misses you most of all. It has been more than five months since you left us, but she still goes to the door every afternoon to call for you with the most heart-wrenching cries. The moment the front door opens, she darts outside to look for you. Sometimes she just sits and stares out of the window, lost and confused. Her loss and loneliness are palpable.

No matter how and when we lose our furry family, their love lasts forever. Thinking of you with love from all the "Eligible Cats in and around Wellington".

Part 2 - My Story
by George Stuart Deane
My First Family

My name is George. I was born on Christmas Eve, 2012, but I can't remember much about that time. My mother was a very young cat herself, or so I am told. She was only seven months old when I and my siblings were born. I came first, and I'm quite a big boy. Mother was a tiny scrap of a cat, and I kept her in labour for many hours. I know it isn't my fault, but I feel awful that she didn't survive the experience: by the time her people realised she was in trouble and took her to the SPCA, it was too late. The vet eased

me from her faltering body and managed to deliver my brother, but my sisters were stillborn. Mother earned her angel wings shortly after.

2012 was a busy kitten season and many nursing queens had been surrendered to the SPCA that year. Luckily, there are many kind volunteers and foster families who provide temporary homes for unwanted cats like me. My own family decided that they didn't want the bother of raising an orphaned kitten and were secretly relieved that my mother had passed away. When they had bought the cute little scrap of fluff on impulse from a pet shop six months earlier, they hadn't considered the possibility of her giving birth to a litter of her own before the year was out. They didn't have a lot of money, and the costs of having Mum spayed had been beyond their means.

And that, dear readers, is how I ended up with the Taylors.

My Second Family

The Taylors were kind people. They were fostering another cat, one just like Mum who had also found herself in the predicament of an unwanted pregnancy before her first birthday. However, unlike Mum, her original family had surrendered her to the SPCA before her labour started, and she had delivered her kittens safely in the consulting rooms. She and her litter of four were now being fostered by the Taylors, and I was placed into the little family to see if she would accept and rear me as her own. Naturally she did: cats are almost always caring mothers who readily accept and nurture kittens not born to them.

My biological brother wasn't as lucky. He had been placed with another family, but he was a sickly, weak little lad. Despite their best efforts, he too flew back to Planet Cat in the first week, leaving me as the only surviving feline member of my first family. I have absolutely no idea who my real dad was, and thus I can't count him as family. I don't have much regard for the humans who allowed Mum to get pregnant in the first place only to discard me, thus I no longer regard them as family.

Life with the Taylors was good. My surrogate cat mum received the best care and nourishment, and therefore had plenty of milk for us. Being a week younger than the other kittens, I was small and had quite a tough time holding my own, but I managed with a little help from Melanie who would find a nipple and latch me on whenever I cried for help.

Melanie is the youngest Taylor daughter, and we lived in a large basket lined with a fluffy brown blanket next to her bed where she watched over us night and day. She often fell asleep with her little hand still dangling into the basket, resting on my surrogate mum's back. I was her favourite and she made sure the other kittens weren't too rough after their eyes and ears opened and they were learning to walk and play. Naturally, I was a week behind in development, but with Melanie looking out for me, I

I even looked like my surrogate family.

too grew and thrived.

I would have loved to stay with the Taylors and become Melanie's own, special cat, but all too soon it was time for us to leave the foster family. Adoptions had been arranged for all of us, and Melanie cried oceans of tears the day she had to say goodbye. I clung to her as tightly as I could, hooking my baby claws into her T Shirt, but it was no use. With a lump in her throat, the SPCA lady prised me out of Melanie's little hands and placed me in a cage with my surrogate mum and siblings.

 At the door, Melanie turned and blew me a last tearful kiss.

 "Goodbye, Podgy. I love you and I won't ever forget you."

I mewed my own little goodbye in response. I didn't mind Podgy, but I was about to be given my big-boy name: George.

I could fit in this.

Meeting My Third Family

After we had all been spayed and neutered, a young woman came to adopt me from the SPCA. We drove up State Highway One along the Kapiti Coast on a glorious, early autumn day in March 2013. The radio was playing, and she was singing along with a song called My Friend George. It was an old Lou Reid song from 1984 and, although she wasn't from that era, she told me how much she enjoyed retro eighties "rock". She turned to me and smiled.

"Yes, that's it, little guy! We'll call you George. How do you like the name George?"

I mewed indifferently. Personally, I would have preferred being Melanie's Podgy, but I didn't seem to have much choice in anything concerning my fate. However I'm a pragmatic sort of cat.

"It'll do," I replied with a little chirp, but she was already singing along to the next song.

I could tell that she didn't understand Catlish. I've found that few people do. Catlish is a sort of dumbed-down Felinese for the benefit of humans, a type of pidgin. Felinese is the noble official language of Planet Cat. It is largely non-vocal: it's the flick of a tail, a twitch of a whisker, the bat of an eyelid or a narrowing of the pupils. These and many other subtle gestures are well beyond the comprehension of mere humans. While there are some sounds in Felinese, these are generally used as accents.

 On the other hand, Catlish is the baby talk kittens use. Adult cats use it merely to communicate with inferior species such as humans. It consists of various meows, squeaks, chirps and even a few body gestures, the least subtle of which can be comprehended by humans. I'm sure you're all familiar with a claw hooked into a tender spot on your thigh, or a well-timed nip, or a swat from a paw with claws sheathed (sometimes unsheathed if the human in question is being particularly obtuse). We get by quite well communicating with humans in this way – if it's a reasonably intelligent human we're dealing with. When we talk among ourselves, we rarely speak Catlish.

The journey up to Paraparaumu was uneventful and my new digs were okay. She put me in a basket which I assumed was to be my bed. I tested the blue blanket for softness by kneading it a little. Yep. It was acceptable.

Kapiti Island from Pukerua Bay.

Her partner was a nondescript human who paid no attention to me whatsoever. If I had been a tea towel, he couldn't have been less interested. He sprawled on the couch clutching a green bottle from which he took regular sips, completely in thrall to a big magic window. When we arrived he barely grunted an acknowledgement to our presence.

Tiny little humans clad in black were running around on a big field outside the magic window trying to steal an elliptical ball from other little humans dressed in green. It went to and fro: first one group would have it and the others would be chasing them, then the other lot would get it and kick it over a weird structure of vertical and horizontal poles.

The scene outside the enchanted window would suddenly change and there'd be a big ugly, boxy motor car covered in mud, inching its way up an impossibly steep slope towards a snow-capped peak, then in a few seconds, the vista would change and we'd be looking into a room full of sweaty people running on machines, going nowhere and frantically pedalling bicycles stuck to the floor.

The blokes would then return and the chase for the elliptical ball would start all over again. I couldn't see the point of any of this. Humans have strange pursuits, and it was all utterly boring to me. I turned around a few times, then curled up and fell asleep in my basket with my back to the magic window.

The Unholy Terror That Screamed All Night and Day

I don't have a lot to say about those early years. There isn't much to discuss, and I'm not a very talkative bloke.

We moved around a lot. Paraparaumu to Levin, Levin to Otaki, Otaki to Paraparaumu and then back to Otaki. I think it had something to do with his job. He was a bland human being, and I had absolutely no connection with him. I can't even remember his name and I'm sure he didn't know mine. You could say that we had a mutual disinterest: he had no interest in me and didn't make the slightest effort to get to know me, and I reciprocated the attitude.

I think her name was Clara or Clare, or something like that. When she was home, which was very seldom in that first year, she wasn't particularly interested in me either. I pretty much had the place to myself, and I'm not sure why they had even wanted to get a cat because they clearly were not cat people. I didn't mind being alone all the time once I got used to entertaining myself. I quite liked the peace and quiet and became very accustomed to it.

So, you would understand my horror when, at the end of that year, she went away for two or three

Melanie who had been so gentle and tender with me. She had been taught from an early age to handle animals with care and respect, and I'm sure it isn't *that* difficult to train little humans. Sadly, most people don't seem to see the necessity of it these days.

As the little terror grew, he became stronger, swifter and more capable of inflicting pain, so as a result, I was seldom home. Wherever we lived, I spent most of my time outdoors and became quite accustomed to it, no matter the weather. I'd slink in very late to eat (even though there was seldom anything in my bowl) and, if it was a really cold or wet night, I'd stay indoors, high up on a cupboard and out of harm's way.

The Yapping Abomination

This was the first five or six years of my life until they got the puppy. I had become acquainted with some very nice dogs living in the neighbourhoods we'd moved to, and some had even shared their dinners with me when my humans forgot to feed me for days at a time. They were very pleasant creatures, and I called them my friends.

After a lovely sun-drenched October day in 2018 which I'd spent outdoors as usual, I snuck inside very late one night in the hope of a quick bite to eat. The place smelled of dog, but not a familiar one. I looked carefully, and there it was, asleep in a box in the corner! I was about to hop back out of the kitchen window when it noticed me and started the most

days and came back with a miniature version of *him,* only *much* worse than the original. It shrieked and wailed non-stop. It kept her so busy that she often forgot to feed me, and I was forced to find my own meals. I soon discovered that earthworms were quite edible, as were the horrible noisy bugs that make a racket all summer long. I am very proud of the number of those things I silenced.

I thought that the stinky miniature human would quieten down in due course, but it never did. Even worse, it learned to move about of its own accord and crept up on me as I was taking naps in my basket. Quite often, I would wake to a shooting stab of pain up my spine as it yanked my tail.

"No, no, Tristan, no ouchy kitty," she'd gurgle at it, but it would simply ignore her. She'd turn back to her phone and leave me to fend it off as best as I could.

I knew that not all human children were this unpleasant. I had fond memories of dear little

The Road to Waikanae

In the first week, I drifted aimlessly about our neighbourhood in Otaki, visiting various friendly houses I had discovered, gleaning whatever I could in the way of food. Of course, I would have preferred to have settled at one of them, spending my days snoozing in the sun on someone's deck or under a daisy bush in a pleasant garden enjoying the fragrance of flowers and the humming of bees. I like gardens, and I'm a good gardener.

This was not to be my destiny, however. It was no more than a faint whisper of a vague feeling at first. I'm unsure when I first became aware of it, but I started feeling the urge to head South. Planet Cat operates a very sophisticated communication network, far superior to any human technology.

To the South, not too far away, another cat already knew that her days on Planet Earth were coming to an end, and that her humans would soon be in need of me. When Planet Cat speaks, you obey: it's as simple as that. Sparky was about to be recalled, and I was being summoned to bring comfort to her fragile humans. They would need every ounce of it I could provide.

So, one morning at the beginning of December 2018, after a long, refreshing sleep under a house on the outskirts of Otaki, I set off for Waikanae. I don't like noise and traffic, so I stayed away from State Highway One as I went. The river Otaki presented my first problem. I'm not a keen swimmer and, as far as I could tell, the easiest way to cross it was via the SH1 bridge.

awful yipping, howling din. I couldn't stand the high-pitched noise, and in my haste to escape, I bumped a glass casserole dish off the counter. It shattered on the floor with an almighty crash.

This set the child off. It had been woken by the puppy's hysterical yipping, but now it ran down the passage to its parents, shrieking loudly. By the time they all came tearing into the kitchen, I was long gone, over the fence and away.

Like a re-run of the child's upbringing, the pup too wasn't taught any manners or social skills. As it grew, it became stronger and bigger and I could no longer hold my own. Coming home to eat was a nightmare that I dreaded. The dog would lay in wait for me and terrorise me the moment I set foot in the house. It was big enough too to nudge my food bowl off the counter when it stood on its hind legs and there was hardly ever anything for me to eat when I came home. There simply was no reason to come home anymore and by late November 2018, I stopped going home altogether.

There was no way I was going to attempt it during the busy daylight hours, so I rested in the shade of a large tree on the bank until sundown.

Finally, it was late enough for the traffic to have died down, save for an occasional freight truck on the last leg into Wellington, bringing supplies for the capital. I watched these monstrous vehicles as they rattled across the bridge, shaking the very earth beneath my feet as I crouched in the darkness a few metres away. It took me a long time to steel myself for the crossing and, just when I thought I was ready, another one would roar past and I'd lose my nerve again.

The first faint light of dawn was starting to spill over the Tararua ranges when I finally gathered my courage. Heart racing, I dashed out of the bushes and onto the verge of the road, sprinting for the bridge's narrow pedestrian walkway.

I ran as if my life depended on it because it most certainly did. I was on that bridge for less than a minute, but it felt like eternity. I could see the tantalising vision of long grass at the end of the bridge. I was nearly there! The air was burning in my throat as my heart thumped with the exertion. Then I heard it. From behind came the sound of rolling thunder, approaching fast. Blind terror made me freeze in my tracks, close my eyes, and resign myself to my fate.

The eighteen-wheeler roared past mere inches from where I was crouched tightly against the barrier rail. The wind of its passing whooshed into me ruffling my fur, almost toppling me. On shaking legs, I trotted the last few metres and dived gratefully into the long grass to the right where I lay for several minutes to compose myself.

A sudden feeling of euphoria flooded over me as the adrenaline subsided and I noticed the beautiful dawn chorus of the birds in the bushes all around me. (One of them would have made a rather tasty

breakfast but I'm afraid I'm not much of a hunter when it comes to birds. They're too fast for me.)

I had just survived the most daring adventure of my life! Feeling like the King of the World, I made my way down the riverbank for a drink. I was still panting from the effort of the last few minutes. I'm not really built for speed. I'm a solid cat, not a sleek or slinky one. I lapped at the water, looked across at the opposite bank where I'd spent most of the previous day, and put in a request to Planet Cat that my journey might be easier now that I had crossed the mighty Otaki. And from the aether, a small, silent voice assured me that I would be safe. My mission was clear, it said.

I resumed my journey, cutting across country towards Te Horo Beach, staying as far from the highway as I could. I made use of the back roads only when I absolutely had to, and I knew that Planet Cat was keeping its word. After the bridge, my travels were uneventful. I found plenty to eat in the form of mice, insects and lizards along the way, as well as the odd meal I scrounged from rubbish bins. The summer months were bountiful, and the weather was good. I was used to living outdoors and enjoyed the freedom of open spaces with the earth under my

feet. The smell of the ocean was always close by.

I took my time, knowing that I wasn't needed just yet. It would be some time before little Sparkles was ready to cross The Rainbow Bridge, after which my services would be needed. I crossed the Mangaone Stream via Sims Road and reached Te Horo Beach two weeks after my near-death experience on the Otaki River bridge. I dawdled there a few days, exploring the vegetation along the fringes of the beach and competing with seagulls for the discards of holidaymakers and fishermen.

In the week after Christmas, it started getting busy at Te Horo Beach. There were many more holidaymakers and day trippers arriving, so I decided to move on. I strolled along the coastline for all of January 2019, making my way to Peka Peka Beach which I reached early in February.

Peka Peka too was much too active for me at this time of year, so I didn't stay long. I knew Sparky wasn't far away but also that it wasn't her time yet, so I cut inland again, leisurely travelling south to Waikanae.

Crossing the streams winding through the area was no trouble at all as they were mostly dry, but eventually I had to face State Highway One again. I was terrified of it after the experience on the bridge, but I made a crazy dash across it late one night near Smithfield Road and all went well. From there, I continued into suburban Waikanae via the Nga Manu Nature Reserve.

"Efforts and courage are not enough without purpose and direction."
- John F. Kennedy

The Little Old Lady

I lived for a while in the cool tranquillity of the Motuiti Reserve, scrounging from the backyards nearby. This was how I found old Mrs. Kingi. She lived by herself in a little house on Ngaio Road, near the shops. As I was sunning myself on the bank at the bottom of her garden one day at the end of March, she came out clutching her walking stick, bent nearly double. I had never seen such an ancient human being.

Instant connection.

She looked directly at me. I must have seemed rather rude as I stared back at her with unabashed fascination but she didn't seem to mind my rudeness. I had learned to keep away from humans and I usually do: I hide as soon as I become aware of them, but this time I was caught off guard.

"Well, well, well! Look at you! You're a fine young fella, aren't you? My old boy, Tom, used to lie in that exact spot sunning himself, God bless his soul," she chuckled, and approached me arthritically.

I perceived the gentle soul of an animal lover, so I stayed put.

"Well? Where do you come from, Handsome?" she asked me, and I blinked slowly at her in reply.

Clearly, she was able to understand Felinese because she smiled and blinked back at me, then asked in English if I'd fancy a snack. I'm not a bloke who turns down a free meal when it's offered, especially in my circumstances, so I followed her to her kitchen doorstep and waited politely to be invited in.

"Come on then! Don't be shy. Come and sit with me while I have my sandwich," and she beckoned as she made her way to the table and lowered herself painfully into the chair. She reached for a knife and carved half of her bacon sandwich into little blocks which she fed me piece by piece while she enjoyed her portion. I was touched by her kindness. It was the most delicious meal I'd had in my life, and I realised that a simple meal offered in kindness is better than the most lavish fare served on a golden plate with indifference.

much minced beef as I could eat. When she had cream in her coffee, I had some in a saucer. We often had roast chicken, and we had fish and chips on Fridays. Most of all, I loved the bacon and eggs she served me at breakfast time. This wasn't the healthiest diet for a cat, I'll admit, but I believed I had earned a little pampering and soon grew rather cuddly.

In return for her kindness, I kept her company through the long, lonely hours of her everyday existence. By day, I would sit beside her in the garden as she enjoyed the sunshine. Then we'd take a little nap on the couch together after lunch. After teatime I'd keep her lap warm, and steady the ball of wool for her when she forced her gnarled fingers to knit. At bedtime, I cuddled up solidly against her thin, arthritic frame and lent her my warmth to ease the pain in her back, all the while keeping up a constant rhythmic purr to soothe her to sleep.

I also discovered bacon, the food of the gods. I knew that Sparky and her people were now close by, and that I could reach them easily. Sparky had a little while left on Planet Earth still. Mrs Kingi, on the other hand, didn't. Planet Cat required me to keep her company until her time came.

I had lost a lot of weight on my trek from Otaki to Waikanae, and Mrs. Kingi set about remedying that. I dined like royalty, sharing every meal with her. She fed me the choicest bits of salmon, and I had as

The catering was up to Planet Cat's standards.

But one morning, Mrs. Kingi didn't wake up. I'd been with her almost three months and had become very fond of her. On that cold June morning, I suddenly realised I could no longer hear the beating of her heart as I lay next to her. Her body was warm under the blankets, but when I wriggled out and sniffed her face, I couldn't feel her breath on my whiskers.

I sat in silence with her, saying my final farewells. I knew something had to be done. Humans have rituals and customs concerning their dead, and someone would have to come and attend to her. I didn't know if she had family because I had never seen any, but I had witnessed her speaking with her neighbours occasionally, so it was up to me to break the terrible news.

It was still early when I wriggled through the cat flap which had once been used by her beloved Tom. She'd told me many stories about him, and by her accounts he was quite an exceptional cat. We all are, aren't we? It is well known that a spirit cannot be blessed with a feline form on earth unless it is indeed exceptional, and I wondered if Tom wasn't sitting at the pearly gates welcoming her to Planet Cat at that very moment. I'm sure he was.

A neighbour came out dressed in his work clothes and I hopped onto the bonnet of his ute.

"Hello, boy, you're out early," he greeted me.

I meowed at him, trying my best to form human words. It came out as a series of meows in Catlish, and all I managed was to get him to stroke my back.

"Meow, meow, owwww, oww," I persisted.

I nipped his hand in frustration, trying to make him understand.

"Ow! What was that in aid of? Don't you like it? Okay, how about this, then?" he said and tickled me under the chin.

I nipped him again, quite hard this time. He seemed taken aback.

"Shoo! Get off, I have to go to work," he said, angrily trying to push me off the ute. I swiped at him, and a thin red scratch appeared on his hand.

"What the hell's wrong with you today, boy?" he asked.

I reached out and dug my claws into his wrist, pulling his hand towards me, but he shook it free and pushed me off. I had no option but to lunge at his ankles and cling to the trouser leg with my teeth in a desperate attempt to tug him towards Mrs. Kingi's house. Humans can be very obtuse, but this one was brighter than most and knew it was not my characteristic behaviour.

"What's up?" he asked again, and again I tried to tell him.

I turned my back on him and walked a few paces towards home, then turned and looked back over my shoulder. He hadn't moved, so I tried again. I tugged at his pants and walked a few paces. Only then did it dawn on him that I wanted him to follow, and he did. I trotted ahead and darted through the cat flap while he knocked on the door. He called and knocked while I leapt up onto the bedside table and picked up her glasses in my mouth. As he was about to turn away, I emerged from the cat flap and dropped the spectacles at his feet. When I saw the look in his eyes, I knew I had finally got through to him and that he understood.

A little later, some men arrived in a van and wheeled her out, covered by a sheet. I watched sadly from the safety of the bushes at the end of the garden, knowing that this was the end of a chapter in my journey.

"*Death is not the opposite of life, but part of it.*"
-Haruki Murukami

Sparky

That day, I made my way through several lush gardens before finding the one I was looking for. A sad little white cat with a banded black and white tail, two black patches on her back and a black patch over each ear sat looking at me through an upstairs window. I sensed her pain and weariness.

"You've come", she communicated through the glass. *"It's time. Not long to go now. I don't want to leave them, you know, but I can't bear it much longer. The pain…*

Humans are such fragile beings. I'm concerned about them, especially him. I hope he will manage without me. I hope he knows I'll be watching over him from up there, but you will have to comfort them down here as best you can. Thank you for coming."

"I'll do my very best," I replied.

I hung back in the garden, not wanting to intrude on Sparky's last days with her human and feline companions. It wasn't as cosy as sharing Mrs. Kingi's warm bed and nice kitchen, but I was quite used to living out of doors, and the garden chair at the patio door was relatively comfortable. If I curled myself into a tight enough ball at night, it wasn't unbearably cold.

A neighbouring cat who had previously regarded the garden as his own befriended me. He knew my presence had been sanctioned by Planet Cat and made no objection to me living in his annexed territory. He would occasionally invite me to his home around the corner to share his biscuits, and for the first time I found an unexpected pleasure in the companionship of a feline friend.

The exclusively indoor cats at the Deane household kept an eye on me. They seemed to accept my presence in their garden, all except the big Calico goddess. I was enthralled by her beauty and found myself in love, but more about that later. All of them knew Sparky's days were numbered, and that I had come to assist with the comforting of the humans after her departure for Planet Cat.

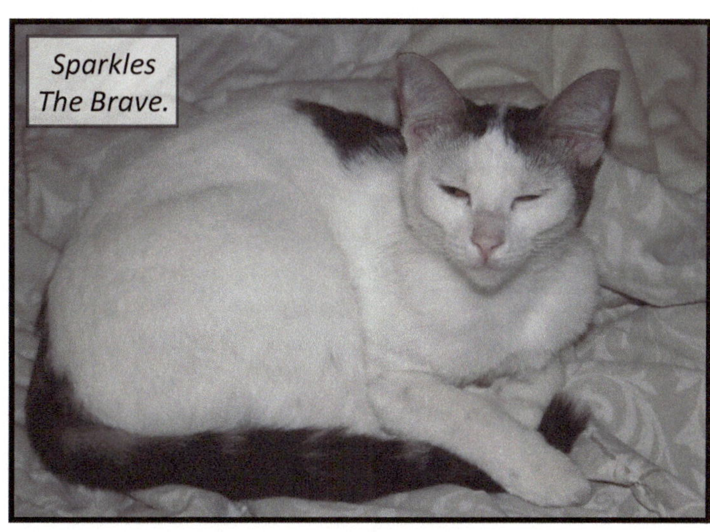

Over time, I made friends with all of them through the windows, but I kept my distance from the sad and troubled humans. They were aware that Sparky was gravely ill, but I wanted them to focus all of their attention on her, and not me.

Then, for the second time in only two weeks, another beautiful spirit departed the physical realm of earth. This time it was a feline soul. Once Sparky's bright essence departed its painful, worn-out little earth body, it hovered for a moment over me in the garden and thanked me again for the service I was about to render. Then she lingered by the window for a final glimpse of the tearful man inside, who was still clinging to her discarded furry shell. As her final farewell, she sent him a wave of such radiating, overwhelming love that we all felt it despite the sadness. Lastly, she fluttered around the other human on the bench outside and beckoned me closer before shooting off with great joy, up, up and away to Planet Cat, finally free of the pain which had shackled her to her body.

"No time on Earth
is long enough to
share with the
animals we love,
or prepare our
hearts to say
goodbye."

Moving in with the Love of My Life

I decided to let the family grieve privately on the first evening. In the morning, I sat under a clump of ferns and watched them dig her little grave, in sight of her favourite window, then lay her earth-suit to rest beneath the soil. I've always found this human custom quite peculiar. Cats know very well that a discarded body is simply that: a piece of earth that must decay and recycle. The real being, the spirit, has no need of its shell after departing the earth for eternity. Humans go to great lengths, sometimes even preserving the shell or its ashes and visiting the place of burial, perhaps believing the spirit lingers there. Nevertheless, as they seem to derive comfort and closure from these rituals, one can hardly begrudge them.

I could feel their heartache.

Mr. Deane returned to his desk and busied himself with work in order to shut out the pain of losing Sparky. Linda dawdled by the grave and planted something fragrant that would continue the cycle of life. I felt it was time to make my move. I sidled up to her and rubbed my flank against her leg. Deep in her world of grief, she reached down absently and stroked my back. Then, startled, she smiled at me through her tears and picked me up.

I don't like being carried as a rule. I feel nervous when I don't have all four paws planted firmly on the ground, but I indulged her and kept perfectly still as I allowed her to wipe her face on my nice clean fur. It would be easy enough to wash all that salty stuff off later. She hugged me tightly and carried me into the house.

I had been called here to bring comfort to the grieving humans and I'd obeyed the summons, but I had no inkling of the reward Planet Cat was about to bestow on me when my feet touched the kitchen floor. That luscious creature glared at me with such passion, and I was blown away by her exotic accent, the intensity and choice of the colourful words she flung at me in her unique Catlish dialect. The last shred of my resistance crumbled, and I fell hopelessly and instantly in love with her. This was Callie, the fiery, colourful goddess of all cats, and the most beautiful being I'd ever seen.

I had no idea what she was saying because I wasn't familiar with her African dialect of Catlish, but the Felinese I understood perfectly. With a saucy sway of her voluptuous hips, she turned her back on me and sashayed out of the kitchen. Her tail was whipping tantalisingly from side to side as it beckoned me to follow, and I knew immediately that she was as enamoured of me as I was of her.

"It's so amazing when someone comes into your life and you expect nothing out of it but suddenly, there right in front of you is everything you'll ever need."

She stopped to glance at me briefly over her shoulder. Her whiskers trembled enticingly. My heart skipped a beat.

Linda was able to lure her back into the kitchen with a hearty meal which we enjoyed together — it was our first date. Afterwards we retreated to the comfortable dining room bar where we lingered over a bowl of refreshing, crystal-clear spring water. There we flirted lightly, trading playful insults before taking a short nap, side by side.

every inch of my gorgeous coat, but she steadfastly scorned me with outbursts in Catlish I could not follow. Every so often, she'd stretch out a luscious leg enticingly and wash it with long, slow strokes of her dainty pink tongue while studiously ignoring me. It was almost more than I could bear.

My beautiful Callie continued to play the coquette for the rest of the day. I tried as hard as I could to impress her with my strong, masculine physique, sitting directly in her line of sight while slowly stretching my muscles and meticulously washing

We enjoyed another refreshing nap on the plush, carpet in front of the lounge windows before moving back to the dining room, following the sun. I understand that this carpet was laid exclusively for the benefit of my queen and her subjects, and I have to say it beats sleeping on a bed of dry leaves or a patch of grass!

When I woke, I stretched luxuriously and smiled at Her Majesty, Queen Calpurrnia the First, tucked neatly in her box a foot away. My heart thrilled at the sight of all that glorious fur-clad flesh, coloured in the most brilliant shades of orange, glossy black and pristine white, in stark contrast with her delicate, fine-boned face, paws and tail.

I was invited to use the outside bathroom several times that day and obliged readily. I am not a litterbox type of bloke and prefer to pee outside. The inside conveniences were for the use of my beautiful queen, her ladies in waiting: Miss Candace and Miss Madelyn, and her page, the little lad Vladimir. I returned promptly after doing my business, and the well-trained human staff were on hand to slide open the patio door.

I wasn't sure why they gifted me a light-weight neck torc inscribed with mysterious human symbols, but assumed it was a token of honour and respect. It wasn't uncomfortable, so I wore it with pride to not offend them.

On my first evening with Sparky's family, I discovered further delights. When I had lived with Clare and the brute, I was not allowed on the furniture. The couch had been for the exclusive use of the beer-swilling, burping man of the house. He spent most of his time slumped on it in a stupor. Mrs Kingi's was a hard old sofa which hadn't been terribly comfortable, so I preferred the warmth of her lap as she knitted in her rocking chair.

However, in the Deane household, couches and beds are for the exclusive benefit of cats, although we graciously permit our human staff to enjoy the opulence with us when they're off duty. Not only were the couches plush and comfortable, but they were covered in thick blankets and cushions to enhance our enjoyment of them. Despite this, my queen preferred to recline on the lap of one of her devoted human servants whenever relaxing in front of the magic window which I now know is called 'television'.

Personally, I can't see the attraction of the magic window, except when there are birds and mice to be viewed on the other side of it. The humans seem to enjoy it, and they sit still for long periods, mesmerised.

This of course means lengthy and comfortable naps for cats, curled up against a warm human thigh, or on a lap if you're Callie and all the laps belong to you by right. For my part, I was quite happy to snuggle up beside Mr. Deane after we had resolved that particular issue.

Once they were done watching, he invited me to

make a quick trip to the outside bathroom, but I declined as I had no need of it. He gave me a bemused look and slid the door shut, locking it securely for the night.

The queen and I dined lavishly, although I was rather disappointed to learn that bacon was not on the menu. Linda and Mr. Deane retired to the servants' quarters on the bedroom side of the house, bearing a tray of food for the other felines and turning the lights out as they went.

Finally, I had the luscious Callie to myself, but she crawled prudishly into her canopied bed in front of the warm blowy thing. On a side note, I rather like this thing. I believe it's called a heater or heat pump or something like that, and it is a very useful device invented by some very clever humans, the purpose of which is to keep their feline masters warm.

I sidled up to Callie's bed and lay down on the carpet beside it, breathing in the intoxicating fragrance of her silky fur emanating from her kitty cave. She fell asleep quickly and I soon drifted off to the music of her deep, sonorous snores, the warm air from the

heater flowing gently over my coat. It was bliss.
What more could a cat possibly ask for? This was
home. Finally.

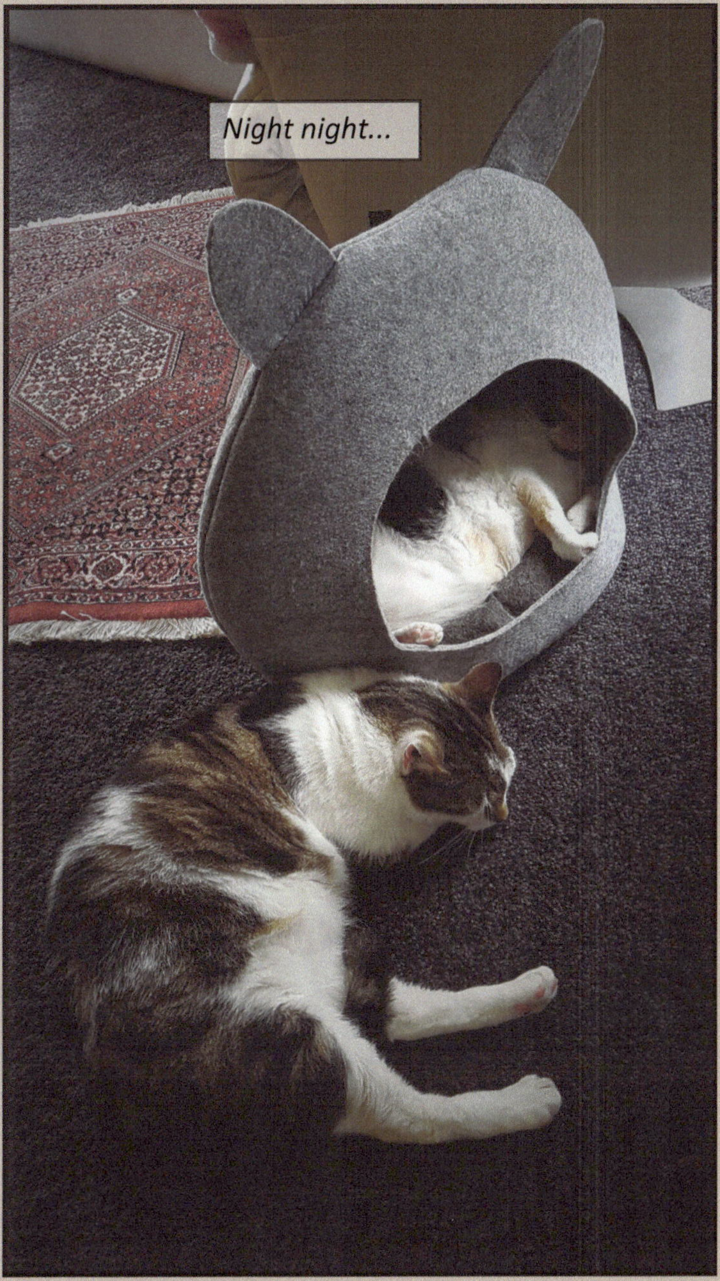

Grave Danger

The next morning, Her Majesty emerged from her cocoon, refreshed and in a very agreeable mood. I approached and we exchanged nose-sniffs. She washed my face and I washed hers. She then proceeded into the kitchen, and I followed. Shortly after, Mr. Deane appeared and we were served

a breakfast befitting our royal status as king and queen of this house, although, again, there was no sign of bacon. I've tried to address this issue on several occasions, but, sadly, humans, can be very imperceptive although useful in other respects. Much as I love my human staff, they are sometimes very, very slow on the uptake. I find Linda and Mr. Deane to be particularly dull-witted, but I'll give them credit for loyalty and devotion.

Later that morning, I had a nasty fright when Linda unceremoniously bundled me into a big plastic box with a handle and a mesh front. I was caught off guard, but by the time I resisted, it was too late and I was securely trapped. They put me in the car and drove off to the vet. I was terrified by not knowing what was going on, but luckily it was nothing more than a quick 'beep'. The vet lady had a device in her hand which scanned my back and neck, and when it beeped at her she seemed quite satisfied. I crawled back into the safety of the box and relaxed as we drove away, sensing that we were going back home.

But the worst was yet to come. I'd only been resident at Castle Deane for a few days when, late one afternoon, a car pulled into the driveway. Out of it peeled The Unholy Terror That Screams All Day and Night and The Yapping Abomination, followed by the people who had adopted me from the SPCA six years before. I was horrified. I had done everything in my power to escape this family. How on earth had they found me? There was no way I wanted anything to do with them again, and so I fled in terror to the only safe place I could find at such short notice.

The child spotted me as I dived behind the couch and came after me, yanking my tail painfully. Callie growled and jumped onto the dining room table as the dog barrelled towards us. Thankfully, she managed to hoist her bulk to relative safety just in time. Hissing and spitting, I suffered the indignity of being dragged out by my back legs by the child. Oh, the embarrassment of suffering this humiliation in front of my queen was almost too much to bear! Luckily, Linda was there to scoop me up and place me out of harm's way on her shoulder.

Mr. Deane tried to make sense of the woman's babbling over the din of the children and the dog, while Linda tried calming them all down. Whatever Mr. Deane said to the woman resulted in them leaving, but not without a fuss from the child. Nevertheless, they left and were never seen again, thank goodness! I purred around Mr. Deane's ankles to show my deep and heartfelt gratitude a short while later, once I'd regained my composure.

But
not
for us.

Fine!

Fine!

Bacon
for
them.

Because
Callie was
rude to
Linda
again.

The benefits
of catnip.

Meeting The Rest of The Family

Shortly after this incident, I was officially introduced to the rest of the household. I'd met them all through the windows when Sparky was still in residence, but Mr. Deane and Linda felt that it was time for the formal introductions.

Candace Marie is known simply as Candy. Mr. Deane calls her Wally or Wallace for reasons I'll explain later, and sometimes The Shoulder-Cat (which will also be explained in due course), and she is a wonderfully loving and affectionate soul with a sunny, open disposition, welcoming of any and all creatures, feline, human and even, to an extent, canine. She was the first allowed into the royal domain (which encompasses the entrance hall, kitchen, lounge, dining room, Mr. Deane's study and the guest bathroom (which houses my Queen's royal commode)) to meet me.

At first, she didn't notice me, and scampered about like a young filly as she sniffed at The Litter Robot (the Queen's commode) and the unused litter tray that had been provided for me. I waited patiently until she finally spotted me and stopped dead in her tracks.

With her tail puffed up coyly, she approached without too much caution, quickly booped noses, sniffed my ears, and that was it. Then she relaxed and continued on her way, enjoying the rare privilege of running amok in the Queen's domain. The Queen herself was less impressed and admonished her with a colourful Catlish diatribe which she simply ignored.

At first glance, Candy is often mistakenly regarded as a bit of an airhead, and I must say that she does do rather silly things from time to time. However, she more than makes up for them with her sparkling and friendly personality. Mr. Deane regards her as a numpty, as do the Deanes' grown-up human children, and they often unkindly refer to her as Wally or Wallace. They also call her Psycho Cat or Bat-Cat, not only for her uncanny resemblance to Batman, but because they think she's crazy. Linda is the only one in her camp and knows better, of course. Candy is anything but crazy or stupid. Candy adores Linda, you see, and Linda adores Candy.

Long before I joined the family, when they lived in South Africa, the bond between Linda and Candy was first formed. Candy was born under a truck to an abandoned housecat who was living semi-feral on busy industrial premises. On the afternoon of 15th December 2014, before she was even a day old, Candy tragically lost her mum when she was run over in the factory yard. The factory owner was distraught. She had been feeding mum, but had no idea how to care for her orphaned litter of four tiny new borns.

Having raised scores in the preceding decades, Linda and her teen daughters were renowned for their ability to hand-rear orphaned kittens. The factory owner called the local vet who contacted the rescue organisations who had Linda and her girls on file as fosterers... and the problem was solved. Surviving the first night alone, Candy, her sister Mia (who I was told looked very much like me), her two ginger brothers, Billy and Tommy were popped into a carrier and driven the 60 kilometres from Pretoria to Johannesburg and handed over to Linda.

Mia was too far gone and earned her angel wings on her first night in the Deane household. Sparky, another orphan who had been taped shut in a box and thrown away, then rescued from the dumpster by Linda's friend Viv (a feral feeder), joined the litter for hand-rearing a week later. I'm rambling on too

The service is great at this bar. I come here often.

much: this is a story for another book which I am informed will be told in due course.

I mention Candy's kittenhood to explain why she is sometimes known as The Shoulder Cat. When they were nothing more than little cat larvae, after each kitten's feed, Linda would put the fed and cleaned kitten on her shoulder as she dealt with the next one. Candy would burrow deep into Linda's neck and continue suckling at her ear until she fell asleep. To this day, she loves being on Linda's shoulder and starts drooling whenever she is there.

Another reason for her nickname is her beautiful little cat-suit which looks just like off-the-shoulder evening wear: one arm and a shoulder is white, while the other is of the purest black.

There is one more reason for this nickname, and it is also what first earned her the 'Wally' moniker. When she was only seven or eight weeks old, she thought it a good idea to sneak out into the courtyard and climb onto the roof, but once up there, she had no idea how to get down and simply took a flying leap off the roof before Linda could rescue her. She landed with a thump in the flower beds below, injuring her shoulder so badly that it had to be strapped up for weeks.

And there you have it: three reasons for Candy being called The Shoulder Cat and reason enough for some to refer to her as Wally the Batty Crazy Cat. Linda's daughters are quite rude and I won't tell you the exact term they use, but the first word is 'bat' and the second rhymes with 'spit'.

On the subject of bats, perhaps it was her Batman mask that inspired her, but Candy took quite a liking to the bats which lived under the eaves of the Deane house, spending hours and hours during the warm African evenings trying to catch them as they emerged at dusk, and waiting all night for them to return before dawn.

Back in those days, the Deanes had twenty resident cats and a number of foster cats and kittens at any given time. All adult cats were allowed outside day and night as the vast property was entirely fenced and cat-proofed. There was plenty of room for everybody and plenty of nooks and crannies to carve out territories between the main house, pool-house, gardens and rockeries. Not a single cat ever escaped their home in Nolene Street, Constantia Kloof, not that I think any would have wanted to! Conversely, no cat managed to break in to that feline fortress either.

Linda had lost too many cats from previous homes to allow her cats access to the outdoors without the protection of an impenetrable boundary fence.

Castle Deane in Waikanae is not fully fenced, and thus all cats live indoors until a proper catio can be constructed. Against her better judgment, I was the only exception. I had proved by my long journey from Otaki that I was able to look after myself.

On arrival in New Zealand, the Deanes brought with them eight cats. Two belonged to their elder daughter and three to the younger. The girls went flatting and took their cats with them, leaving Linda with an empty nest. It had been decades since she'd had only three cats, so when she spotted the beautiful Miss Madelyn on the Outpawed Facebook page, she tried her best to resist temptation.

However, after a month, when Maddy was still available, Linda got in touch with Vikki from Outpawed in Whitby. I'm sure you can guess what happened next. No? Read on, my friend, read on.

Linda went to fetch Maddy, but Mr. Deane prevailed on her to take Vlad home with them too. Initially, Vlad and the gorgeous Moppy were taken in by the Deanes as part of Outpawed's 'Foster To Adopt' programme, but who are we kidding here? The outcome was always going to be adoption.

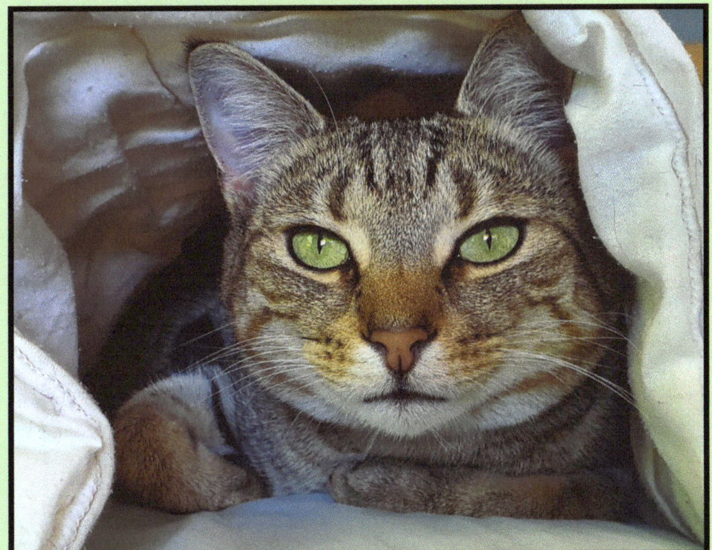

Soon after meeting the gregarious Candy, I was introduced to the Outpawed kids, who by this time had been part of the Deane family for a year-and-a-half. Moppy was very shy. She simply hissed softly at me and scampered back into the peasant quarters, but Vlad threw a hissy fit and screamed at me, puffing himself up as best he could. It was rather amusing, and I tried hard not to laugh at him.

He is a tad insecure. I suppose it has a lot to do with his puny physique. He's not a robust bloke like me. I think it also has something to do with the fact that the Deanes chose Moppy specifically (Linda has a bit of a thing for calicoes, you see) and Vlad was never planned.

He took a liking to Mr. Deane when they came for Moppy, and he cried and cried when Mr. Deane tried to put him down when they were leaving. He begged to be taken home with them too, clinging pitifully to Mr Deane. In his own mind, he is an afterthought and has never really come to terms with it. They refer to him as their problem child, and he vents his insecurity by bullying Moppy.

PS: I forgot to tell you Candy's other nickname. Mr. Deane calls her Liz, as in Liz Hurley, because she has trouble keeping her breakfast down sometimes. Whenever she's excited, up it comes all over the carpets/beds/chairs etc. When this happens, Mr. Deane's standard response is to find Linda and break the news: "Your Shoulder Cat has hurled in the bedroom/lounge/kitchen etc."

Mr. Deane does not do puke, pee or poo, the three sacred Ps of cat servitude. He has the important job of earning the bacon (although I have not seen much of it in this household), while Linda attends to domestic operations.

Vlad has a rather disconcerting habit of nicking items from the laundry basket, particularly undergarments.

My Daily Life at Castle Deane

I'd like to tell you a little about my responsibilities at Castle Deane. As the royal consort to Queen Calpurrnia, I did not consider it beneath my dignity to lend a hand, and I made it my personal responsibility to supervise Linda in the garden. This was necessary as she is not a very competent gardener. I had to keep an eye on her all the time. She had no clue how to dig holes and I constantly had to show her how. Sadly, she still hasn't got the hang of it.I also caught her on numerous occasions ripping up plants, roots and all. I had to put a stop to this with a bodily protest: lying down on the patch of plants she was decimating. Had I not done so, there would not have been a single Dandelion, Dock, Clover, Chickweed or Mallow to grace that garden. Much as I love her, Linda is not the sharpest tool in the shed.

On the subject of intelligence, Mr. Deane is not overly gifted either. To get him to budge from his desk when it is time for a snack, one has to literally reach up onto his chair and dig a claw or two into his

thigh. This usually has the desired effect, and he responds with: "Ouch! Dammit, George, what do you want?" It's unfortunate that I have to resort to incentives of this nature, but it's the only effective way of communicating with the man.

I've heard a rumour that this is a common flaw in most human males. Other than this, Mr. Deane is quite alright and I'm rather fond of him. We blokes have an obligation to look out for each other in a female-dominated establishment such as Castle Deane. Vlad doesn't really count as he's still deciding his gender identity and, in my opinion, behaves more like a girl than a lad most of the time. Yes, I know I'm not being politically correct, but I'm a cat and march to my own drum. I don't care much for human dictates and taboos.

Another task I took on was the protection of Linda whenever she collected the mail, just as I did any time she was out of doors. This task was fraught with

danger. Prior to my arrival, Cocoa, the deranged, unstable brown tabby from next door had assigned herself the task of accompanying Linda to the mailbox, but when I moved in, she was overcome with fits of jealous rage. She had been coveting a spot at Castle Deane for a long time and was very resentful that I'd got in so effortlessly.

 She took it on herself to launch unprovoked surprise attacks on Linda's ankles and feet from the cover of the hedge as she walked down the driveway, and I was the only one who could put a stop to it. I made it my personal duty to lead Linda in safety to the mailbox and back each day.

Cocoa and I were not the best of friends. We had a truce, the terms of which stipulated that she was never to venture into my garden. In return, I would respect her boundaries. There's good reason for Cocoa not being welcome at Castle Deane. Before I came, she would invade the precincts of the Castle, often launching herself at the windows in challenge to Callie and the others, engaging in swearing duels. Sometimes she'd escape the confines of her own home during the darkest hours of the night to provoke them thus. Being woken up this way was particularly terrifying for the Deanes.

When she writes her own book, Callie will tell you about the time Cocoa postured at the window beside the front door. She had provoked Callie from her safe position outside the glass pane until the

Deanes could take it no longer. Linda opened the door with the intention of asking Cocoa politely to go home. The Queen told me that she had gone barrelling out, past the unsuspecting Linda and launched herself like a Sumo wrestler at her cocky but diminutive foe. Cocoa's bravado evaporated instantly at the prospect of direct contact with The Mighty Callosaurus.

Candy too has a tale to tell of how she sent Cocoa scurrying away across the roof after she tried to break in through an upstairs window. The Deane girls are fierce, I have to admit. I wouldn't advise taking them on in their own territory.

I mention Cocoa to illustrate how essential it was that the human inhabitants of Castle Deane had

protection. As the Alpha male of the establishment, I spent most of my time at my post (a conveniently placed, comfortably cushioned garden chair at the patio door) guarding the entrance. I can't say that I never dozed off because it was an exhausting, full-time job, but I always napped with one eye open, constantly on the lookout for that temperamental tabby trespasser. When my Queen was allowed out for a little fresh air, I was particularly vigilant.

When I came inside each day, my Queen gave me a tongue lashing. Unfortunately, I wasn't able to be in two places at the same time, and she made it clear she was none too pleased at being neglected. I told her I had to prioritise household security by day when Cocoa was on the prowl, but when Cocoa was securely ensconced inside her own home at night, I could relax and more than make up for it. Thus, I served my Queen faithfully as her consort and devoted slave. I loved my beautiful Callie with every fibre of my being. We took great pride in our work as we groomed each other from ear to tail tip, multiple times a day. We cuddled up together at night and kept each other cosy. We dined together, often leaning over to sample morsels from each other's plates. Sadly, these morsels never included bacon. I admit to occasionally having to bring my Queen back to earth whenever she got out of hand.

I believe all females tend to do this from time to time, and one needs to be firm but kind in these situations. As you know, the Lady has quite a mouth on her. For the most part, I enjoyed her feistiness and the cussing in her delectable foreign accent, but sometimes it did become excessive. At times like these, I would simply reach out and push her down, then she'd realise her error instantly. Her contrition was most endearing, and we would smooch, purr and cuddle as we reconciled, then snuggle up together for a nap in the sun, or in front of the warm blowy thing.

"Marriage is all about finding that one special person you want to annoy for the rest of your life."

George!

That's disgusting!

Ewwww!

I suppose you've been eating cicadas again?

"Oh, George, I love you more than all the bacon money can buy!"

How come she gets served break- fast in bed, Linda?

The Foster Kids and The Guests

Linda has a faulty off-switch when it comes to cats. As a result, we often had feline guests and foster felines staying with us. My Queen told me that it reached a peak before they all came to New Zealand, but that is a story for another day, and probably another book.

During the time of my residence, old man Harry would visit over Christmas for little vacations away from his demanding family, who in turn would be given time off for a vacation of their own. His first stay marked the advent of Maddie and Vlad. Harry was a dear old chap in his twilight years – and a diabetic. He couldn't simply book a holiday in a cattery like most cats: he needed insulin injections twice a day, so he came to Castle Deane for his holidays where Linda attended to his every need.

When he arrived, she made him comfortable in the spare room for a day or two to settle in, after which he was given the run of the house, excluding the royal quarters, of course. Harry hung with the peasants. He took quite a liking to the large bed in the main bedroom

and made himself comfortable there with Linda, Mr. Deane and the others, while the Queen and I enjoyed the privacy of our side of the house.

Harry's nephew, Bucky, a beautiful young mini panther visited one Christmas. We had quite a crowded house that year. Mulu, another void, and her family of naughty boy kittens were also temporarily in residence, so Callie and I graciously agreed to let Bucky share our quarters during his vacation. This was around the time that Judi joined the family as a stray/foster, and I'll tell you about her in the next chapter.

My doppelganger neighbourhood friend.

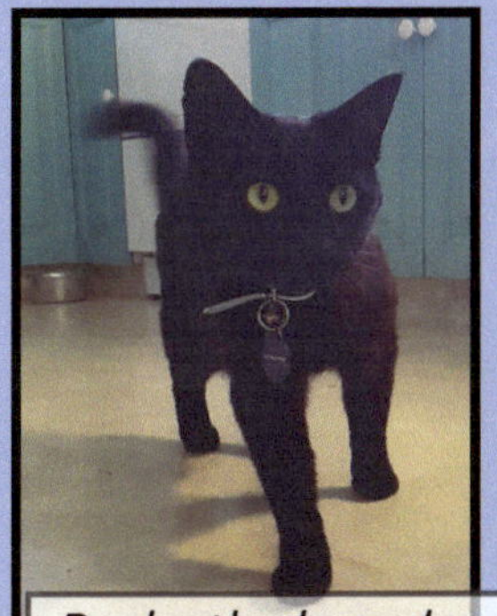

Bucky the boarder making himself comfortable in the royal quarters.

Young Mulu was surrendered to Forgotten Felines Foundation when her family decided that she and her kittens were surplus to requirements immediately after she had given birth. I despair of the human race sometimes: this unnecessary cruelty and their heartless rejection could quite easily have been prevented had they simply invested in a little surgical procedure before she fell pregnant.

Mulu and her kids took up residence in the guest room as Linda's foster project of the season. Uncharacteristically, Linda managed to complete this one without failing as she had done on many occasions, three of which I will tell you about. Had

it not been for Juli forming an instant connection with Mulu, the Deanes would have foster-failed again. To be fair, if it had happened on this particular occasion, it would have been Mr. Deane's fault: he was the one secretly wanting to keep Mulu.

Soon after arriving, Mulu learned to open doors and was therefore given the run of the peasant quarters. Linda devised a barrier for the doorway of the kitten room which the kittens could not yet climb over. Mulu fitted in immediately and got on with all the girls very well, but Vlad, as usual, behaved like the little insecure drama queen he is. Candy and Moppy used to visit the kitten room to babysit and entertain the kids when Mulu needed a break.

Peace reigned until Mulu's boys learned to clamber over the barrier, after which it became a free for all with cats and kittens everywhere. Then Hurricane Judi made her grand entrance and led the boys into new levels of mischief, which I will return to in a minute.

This story had a happy outcome. Linda found Mulu the perfect home with a veterinary surgeon from Brazil, now living in Wellington, and it was love at first sight when Juli came over to meet Mulu. Juli adopted her from Forgotten Felines Foundation and renamed her Freya. The two of them have a beautiful, inseparable soul connection, and Freya lives the life of a princess with her human companions Juliana and Matt, as well as her new feline ones, Loki and Hella.

Before Freya moved out, all her kittens were homed. Linda's friend of many years, Diana, adopted one of them and called him Salem. Two more were adopted to a lovely man called Peter who Linda had found via the Cats of Wellington Facebook group, and Mary from Forgotten Felines Foundation found a family willing to adopt the fourth little chap. All the boys were neutered – and Freya spayed – by Forgotten Felines Foundation (the organisation who rescued them and managed the process) before they left.

All this talk of visitors wouldn't be complete without mentioning Maggie and Pan, or Nippy, Noel and Skippy, the feline grandchildren who live with the Deanes' two grown-up daughters. When the human family came to New Zealand, they brought the feline family members too: Sparky, Callie, Candy, Maggie, Pan, Nippy, Skippy and Noel. The grand-cats are regular visitors whenever they need a break from the girls, and graciously allow their humans to explore New Zealand in return for being waited on hand and foot by Linda at Hotel Deane.

The service
here is
appalling!

Not
even a
hint
of
bacon.

The New Kids

On February 8th 2020, Hurricane Judi slammed into the Deane establishment with a force not experienced before or since. We already had a full house with Mulu and her Mooligans, as Callie and I had named them because they were such incredibly naughty little lads. Linda said they were the naughtiest foster kittens she had ever cared for, but this was before she had met Judi.

Judi simply blew in off the street into a Waikanae hairdressing salon one day in January. Mary from Forgotten Felines Foundation was called to rescue the hairdresser from this furry little eight-week-old tyrant who was loudly proclaiming her status as the Master Cat. She lived with Mary and Frank for a short while, but they also had a full house because kitten season is always a busy time for them.

The green-eyed, snow-white Judi was completely deaf. Up to 22% of green-eyed, white-haired cats are congenitally deaf*, so she could not be adopted out to just anyone. She needed to be an indoor cat, and Mary was unable to find a suitable home. She wanted to keep her, but some of her older resident cats did not take kindly to the white whirlwind tearing up their house and things were not heading in the right direction, so Linda innocently volunteered to foster until permanent accommodation could be found.

Judi took immediate command of everything and everyone, especially the squad of Mooligans whom she led in a push to redefine all limits. The five of them were a destructive force which left the humans reeling but constantly entertained. Judi and her team of little vandals chewed and destroyed cell phone charger cables, bedside lamps, spectacles, and miscellaneous other non-essential items such as the TV remote and the bath plug.

They were intensely sporty, excelling in Curtain Climbing and Elephant Games. Elephant Games is a panoply of sporting events held only in the dead of night. There are no rules, but matches commence after humans fall asleep, and additional points are awarded if they are verified as being in a deep slumber. It's a contest in which the individual who makes the greatest racket by any means necessary is judged the winner.

* The likelihood rises to 40% for an all-white cat with a single blue eye, and upwards of 65% - 85% for an all-white with both eyes blue.

Judi and the Mooligans threw themselves wholeheartedly into every night's contest. They raced up and down the stairs like a herd of elephants, then stomped and pounded in the upstairs room directly above the bed on which the Deanes, Candy, Moppy, Vlad and Mulu were trying to get some rest. They bowled and thudded at full speed into the wooden doors and cupboards sounding like an indoor thunder storm until Mr. Deane would leap out of bed and yell, "Can't you lock those bloody cats up in the spare room so that we can get some sleep?"

This usually signalled the end of the first match which was always won by Judi.

Linda would then attempt to catch them one by one and tuck them away in the guest room. As you can imagine, this was regarded as a challenge by Judi and her team. It took ages for Linda to accomplish,

Yet again, Judi takes the gold! Salem claims silver and the bronze goes to Bob.

and didn't really serve much of a purpose. As soon as Linda was back in bed with the light off, Vlad would immediately go upstairs to free them and the games would resume. Despite his insecurities, Vlad is a gifted athlete himself and an escape artist who had learned to open doors. He could see no reason why the youngsters shouldn't be allowed to practise their nocturnal sport, and the tournament would continue unabated.

Bathroom sport was another favourite. Judi and the Mooligans wreaked havoc in Linda's bathroom if the door happened to be left open. Apparently, bathroom counters should always be clear of all impediments

including toothbrushes, hairbrushes, face cream, hairdryers, make-up, hair products, soap dispensers and the like. All these items should be batted off to lie in a messy jumble on the floor together with towels pulled from rails, contents of tipped laundry baskets and wastebins and shredded toilet paper, so that sprints and other gymnastics may be undertaken on the long counter.

The bath was used as a slide, and because the Deanes hadn't replaced a leaky tap washer, the constant drip was a great source of entertainment with the added bonus of being able to create wet footprint art on the mess lying on the bathroom floor. Bath-plug Soccer was also a regular activity. Imagine Linda's frustration at the end of a long, exhausting day of cleaning up after kittens and serving cats,

when all she wanted was to take a relaxing soak in the tub and the bathplug was nowhere to be found...

Things settled down a little as the Mooligans, and eventually Mulu herself, left for their new homes and Judi ran out of competitors. By this stage, she had cemented her position as the Master Cat, and the humans bowed down to her. Note that this position did not supersede my position as King, nor Callie's as Queen: Planet Cat operates a very complex system of governance which humans cannot comprehend. All cats are supreme rulers in their own right, irrespective of titles, but Judi was indeed appointed to the position of Master Cat. To clarify, Candy is the CEO, Moppy is the Commander in Chief and Vlad is the Executive Vice-President, but don't exert yourselves too much trying to work it all out.

Before we move on to the next set of newbies, I'd like to tell you one or two things more about Judi. I think you might be interested in hearing about how she got her name. Forgotten Felines Foundation have a scheme under which any member of the public can sponsor a rescue. Among other things, this bestows the right to name. The nice lady (The Fairy Cat Mother with the magic spade), Annette a.k.a. The Cat Fixer from Feline Fix (and Ronnie's mum), kindly sponsored Judi and named her after her bestie.

After Mulu had left to start her new kitten-free life as Freya, the Deanes formally adopted Judi, thereby "foster failing" for the umpteenth time. They retained Judi's first name as they liked it very much, and since Mr Deane had taken quite a liking to her and she to him. Mr Deane's first name is Jon. He is of Viking ancestry, and since Judi is his special little snow cat, Linda tacked on the surname 'Jonsdottir'. Mr Deane has a thing for white cats. Although his previous mostly-white Master Cat, Sparky, was closely bonded to him, Judi did not replace or supplant her: she simply stepped into the continuation of the role. Again, don't trouble yourself by trying to grasp how this works: it's part of Planet Cat's grand design, and unfathomable to the inferior human intellect.

Shortly after the events with Mulu and The Mooligans, the whole world erupted into the hysteria surrounding Covid-19. The country was placed into an extensive lockdown, and all humans were forced to stay home, venturing out only for essential purposes. All but the most vital veterinary services were held to be non-essential, and of course Planet Cat bestowed hormonal maturity on Judi Jonsdottir at precisely this time. The Deanes had been planning her spay at the beginning of April, but this was now deemed impossible by the powers that be.

Lockdown progressed uneventfully for the Deanes as they both worked from home. Then Judi decided she needed suitors. As a totally deaf cat, she had no idea what her voice sounded like nor how loud it was. She moved from room to room, shrieking at the top of her voice for all the neighbourhood toms, and posing seductively at the windows. This went on night and day for the final week of lockdown one, and nearly drove us all insane. I'd have gladly obliged the young lady if I thought it would satisfy her in any way, but having been relieved of my own trouble nuggets by the SPCA years before, I knew I'd be unable to assist her. Thankfully, she was spayed after her first heat ended, and (relative) peace and quiet returned to the Deane household.

But Planet Cat was not done with us in 2020. Linda got to hear of a tragedy near Levin. A lovely cat now known as Bronte found herself living "feral" with a

Just fuelling up for the day's work.

large litter of girl kittens to fend for. In her desperate search for food, she survived an encounter with a nasty trap intended to kill smaller animals such as possums, but she and one of her kittens were injured so badly that they needed surgery. Mary from Forgotten Felines Foundation was able to capture Bronte and the injured kitten and rush them to the vet. Bronte had some of her toes amputated and the kitten's leg was damaged irreparably. The only option was to amputate at the hip. Forgotten Felines Foundation managed to raise the $2,500 required for this. In the meantime, one by one, Mary managed to rescue all the kittens except one who remained elusive.

Mum and the injured kitten made a good recovery under the expert care of Mary and her team of vets and, after several weeks of dogged persistence, the last remaining kitten was trapped. By this stage, she had become extremely feral and mistrusting of humans. Can you blame her for her overabundance of caution, having had to fend for herself from the age of about 6 or 7 weeks and witnessing what had befallen her mother and sister, then having her siblings disappear one by one?

All were taken to be spayed. Immediately after their surgery on June 29th, Mary dropped off the amputee and the wild one with Linda for fostering. Mum cat and one of her kittens went to live with

a lovely lady in Raumati where she was given the beautiful name of Bronte Aoife. The kitten was christened Hazel Olive. The remaining sibling went to another lovely lady for fostering.

Although they already had names given by their sponsors, the Deane fosters were immediately dubbed Poddy and Quaddy. Mr Deane thinks this is funny, but Linda does not. She would dearly loved to have blessed them with elegant names like their mother, but Poddy the tripod and Quaddy the four-legged wildling were only meant to stay until Linda could tame Quaddy sufficiently to re-home her and

until she was sure Poddy could cope with only three legs.

Predictably, the Deanes fell in love with them and soon realised that their home was the very best place for a three-legged cat and a wild one who would in all likelihood never learn to fully trust human beings. Thus, Poddy and Quaddy were formally adopted, and the Deanes failed at fostering yet again.

Try as she might, Linda could not get Mr. Deane to budge, and the names Poddy and Quaddy stuck. Linda is a pragmatist who knows how to pick her battles, so she let the matter rest. She had faced this problem with her dad many, many years ago when she had gained her first officially owned and beloved cat, and a name is far less important than being able to call a cat your own. I'm sure you'll hear more about that story in a later book.

Poddy and Quaddy took up residence in the peasant quarters alongside Candy, Moppy, Vlad and Judi. We now outnumbered the humans four to one. They formed, a very streamlined body of staff indeed. Luckily, that side of the house is quite spacious, and

the Queen and I continued to enjoy the relative peace of the royal domain. Poddy soon became quite tame. She loves to cuddle up on Linda's feet at night where she very effectively hampers her sleep patterns. She uses a short, sharp nip to incentivise Mr. Deane to skritch her under her right ear whenever necessary. He very obligingly performs the function of her missing hind leg, although his fingernails are not as sharp as her foot needles.

Quaddy remains very standoffish and does not allow anyone to touch her. She spends most of her time under the bed or behind the curtains. However, she does love it when Mr. Deane breaks out the treats before bedtime, and waits eagerly outside the bathroom door while he takes his shower and cleans his teeth. He's very generous with the Temptations,

far more so than Linda. Mr. Deane has made great progress with Quaddy as a result of that. He aspires to have her cuddle up to him some day as readily as she does with Judi.

Poddy and Quaddy both adore Judi because she took them under her wing from their very first day with us, and the three of them have a deep and inspiring friendship.

Nixie joined the family on February 2nd 2021. She had been spotted in the middle of State Highway One near Johnsonville by Libby and her

family in their car. They managed to stop the traffic, rescued the petrified tabby kitten and took her to Wellington SPCA. Euthanasia was considerd the only option but Libby put out a Facebook appeal. Naturally, this tugged at Linda's heartstrings, and she volunteered to look after the little one until Libby could decide what to do.

The SPCA agreed to release her on condition that they could spay her, and she was handed back to Libby after surgery and driven straight to Waikanae. Libby named her Phoenix for having had not one, but two, close brushes with death.

Linda intended to foster Nixie until she was tame enough to be homed. Needless to say, this never came to pass because Linda failed at fostering again, using the excuse that Nixie wasn't ready to be handled. This was true. To this day, Nixie will only allow Linda to handle her, but on her own terms. She will approach Linda and very occasionally Mr. Deane for attention if she wants it, but does not allow the converse and scampers off the moment anyone makes a move in her direction. You have to respect a cat living life on her own terms, subject to the whims of no human.

There is a lot more I could tell you about all my companion cats, and a veritable treasure-trove of information I've gleaned about the Deane household from before my time with them. Some of these stories go back decades to the South African days, and to the time when Linda first realised she was an ailurophile. But this book is almost full, and all these stories will have to be told by others. This is my story, and I'll close it with a final chapter about my time on Planet Earth.

"No amount of time can erase the memory of a good cat, and no amount of masking tape can ever totally remove his fur from your couch."

- Leo Dworken

Callie and I Don't Agree on Everything...

...But Most of the Time, We Do.

When Cocoa Comes Into *MY* Garden

Sometimes I Just Stay Indoors...

...Because when I *DO* Go Outside, I Get Blamed for Stuff...

First Comms with Gina

I can't say exactly when I first became aware of them. The signals were very vague, but I began picking up messages from Planet Cat around April or May of 2021. Somewhere, not far away, a tiny, fluffy minion of Planet Cat was suffering a terrible ordeal, and the Grand Council had earmarked Castle Deane for her refuge. At first, I didn't realise I would

be leaving before her arrival, and that her express mission was to provide comfort for the humans, just as I had so recently done during Sparky's departure, but Planet Cat gently guided me into preparing for the events about to unfold.

I didn't know the specifics, and I can't say I was overly thrilled to be leaving my family so soon after finding them, but Planet Cat has greater plans for all of us. We cannot alter the preordained, and I had to reconcile myself to saying goodbye to the love of my life, my gorgeous, voluptuous goddess Calico Queen, the luscious Callie.

The signals from Planet Cat's tiny agent grew stronger as May turned into June. I knew she would be arriving soon, just as Sparky had known of my coming and had called out when she knew her time was near. My strongest wish was that this little one would be known by my name because I do not want to be forgotten. I asked her to tell them that she should be called Georgina. She agreed without hesitation and swore to love and protect my humans just as I had done.

On the morning of June 9th, 2021, I went about my business. Before I left for my regular outdoor patrol my beautiful Queen washed my face with such tenderness. I kissed her back with all my love and devotion and almost changed my mind about going out. Little did she know that I wouldn't be coming back. Neither did the Deanes, or they would not have opened the door to let me go.

Most of the day was uneventful. Callie blew kisses at me through the window as she usually does when I'm on patrol, and later, as I settled at my post on the garden chair beside the door, she lay inside sunning herself and we eyed each other amiably through the glass. When Linda came out to collect mail at midday, I accompanied her on our daily hazardous mission. She bent to stroke my back before stepping inside, and I can still feel the love and warmth of her final touch even though I've long since vacated my earthly body.

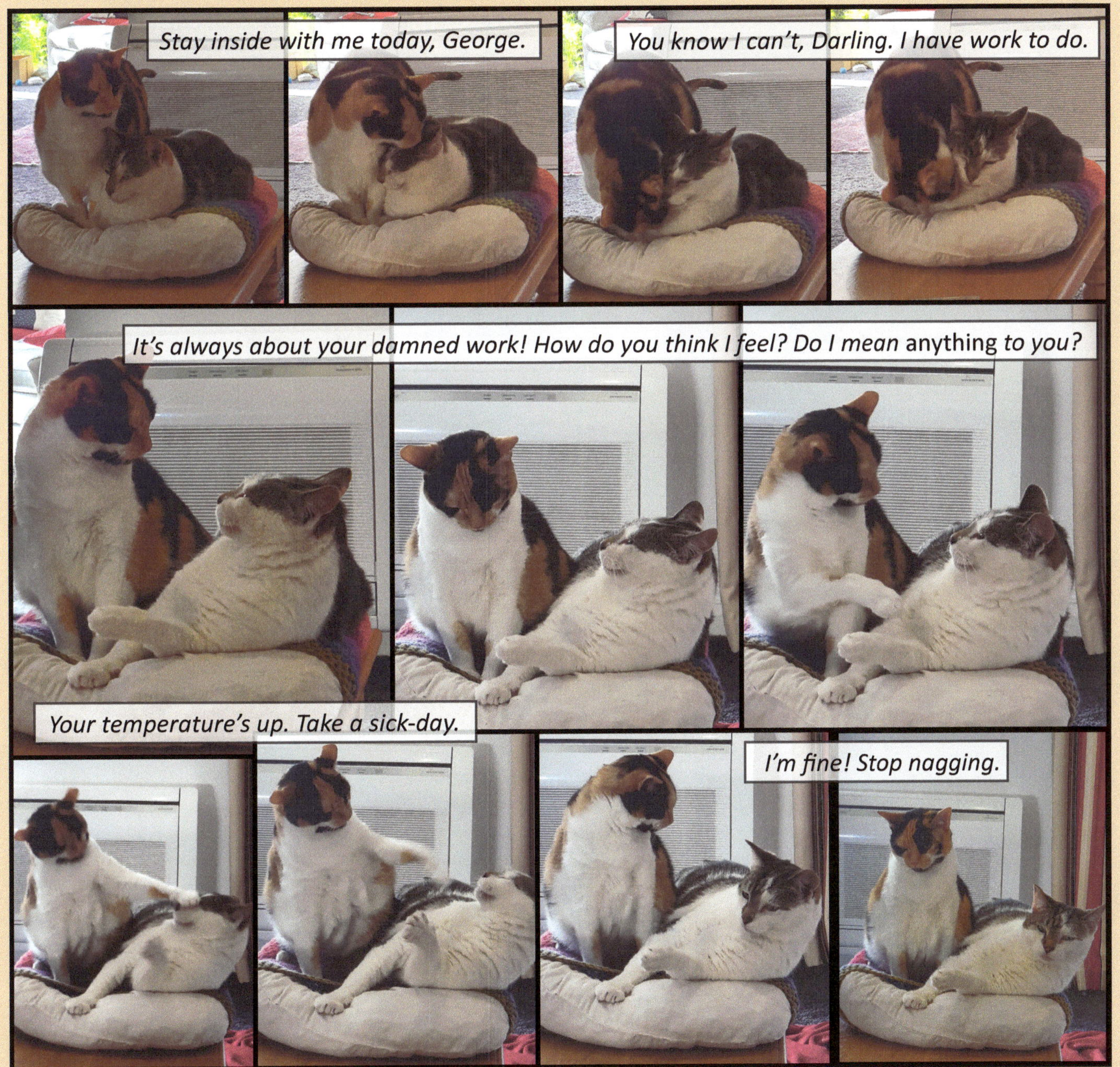

> "I have looked at you in millions of ways and I have loved you in each."
>
> *Haiku (via aesthesos)*

Mr. Deane was busying himself with something in the garage after lunch and I lay watching him from the warm, tarred forecourt. He smiled at me briefly before shutting the garage door and going back inside to his office. The sun was at the perfect angle to catch some rays on top of the fence, and I decided to get up there for my afternoon sunbathe while surveying the four properties bordering this cozy, sheltered spot.

The fence was tricky to climb from the Deanes' side and I had to wriggle underneath it. This was a difficult operation in itself, especially for a solidly built bloke like me but, once through, it was an easy path to the top.

I didn't notice him, the man with the heavy steel-capped boots. If I had, I would have squirmed back and run for the safety of home. I'd survived more than one near miss from those boots, but not today. A blinding flash of white-hot pain exploded at the base of my skull for a second, then everything went black. Almost instantly, the pain was replaced with a feeling of intense rapture and light returned. It surrounded me, bright, shining, and iridescent, in colours I had never seen and simply can't describe in any language. Sparky, shimmering brightly, hovered just beyond my reach with many others whom I have subsequently befriended. These were Romeow, Juliet, Shammy, Picatso, Einstein, Misty and all the other Deane cats who had already transcended time and space.

They allowed me a few moments to say my last goodbyes to those still trapped on Earth.

I visited Mr. Deane in his office where he sat with a headset, absorbed in earnest conversation with colleagues across the world, resolving a complex data technology issue. He paused, staring uncomprehendingly in my direction. He didn't seem to register that I was saying goodbye and continued with his meeting. Linda was also glued to her screen, making entries in her Eligible Cats book distribution database. She felt my presence as a warm, inexplicable feeling but didn't comprehend it. Being closer to the spirit realm, the feline residents all recognised me and bade me farewell.

Finally, I hovered at the dining room window where my Callie lay snoring in the sun. Her dreams took a very pleasant turn as my spirit form tickled her soul. She rolled over contentedly and stretched her magnificent body before realising I was there to say goodbye. I had to tear myself away with her final words ringing in my ears: "Don't leave me, George! Your angel wings were ready, but my heart isn't!"

However, once you are called, it is impossible to stay. I love her and watch over her now from just beyond the limits of the material dimension. Despite her deep sadness that I'm tangibly beyond her reach, Callie knows I'm merely a breath away. She's aware that I am waiting for the moment she is awarded her own wings, and I can only hope and pray that with time, the pain of physical separation will fade, and that the knowledge of our ultimate reunion will bring her hope and comfort.

Before my awareness of Earth's constraints faded completely, I sensed the little Agent Gina Ginger Knickers waving her goodbyes too and asking me to convey her best wishes to all at the spirit world of Planet Cat. She implored me to make sure she made it safely to the Deane household, which of course she did on June 14th, five days later, thanks to Laura from Found-A-Feline.

Feline Fix is a not-for-profit organisation founded in September 2019 by two long-time animal charity volunteers. All too often we've seen the result of unwanted litters becoming a community problem. Some of these kittens are irresponsibly rehomed. At best, they will find their way to an animal shelter where — if it is not too late — they can be socialised and rehomed. At worst, these innocent animals will be forced to lead short lives filled with misery and hardship.

We want to "fix" this problem before it occurs! Quite often it simply comes down to a lack of finance to help us educate on how soon young cats can breed which leads to a failure to de-sex in time. Female cats as young as four months are fertile! Allowing that first litter means that the problem grows exponentially — and the sad cycle continues.

Spaying (female) and neutering (male) cats provides a significant boost to animal welfare. It is our goal to help anyone in financial difficulty de-sex (or "fix") their cats before they have a chance to breed, thereby preventing the problems of unwanted, neglected and abandoned cats.

Feline Fix needs to raise as much money as possible: it will enable us to get our message out and as many cats de-sexed as funds allow. There are countless unwanted kittens and cats living rough on our streets and the Rescue Centres are overflowing with those awaiting their forever homes. It shouldn't be like this!

Contact: **felinefix.kapiti@gmail.com**
Annette 027 2302024 Sandra 021 1086359
Bank acc: 03-0732-0042273-00
or **givealittle.co.nz/cause/feline-fix**
facebook.com/ronniesmum2019

www.ingramcontent.com/pod-product-compliance
Lightning Source LLC
Chambersburg PA
CBHW042113030726
47599CB00002B/201